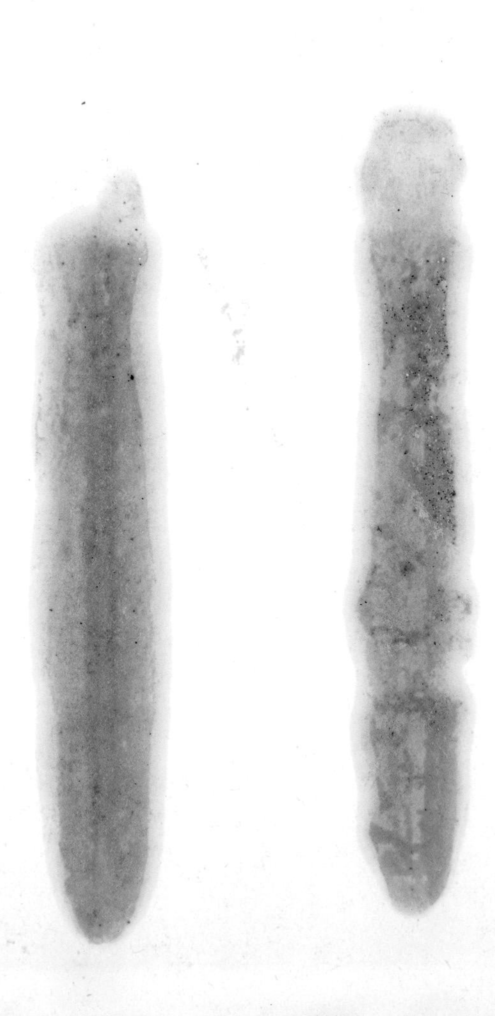

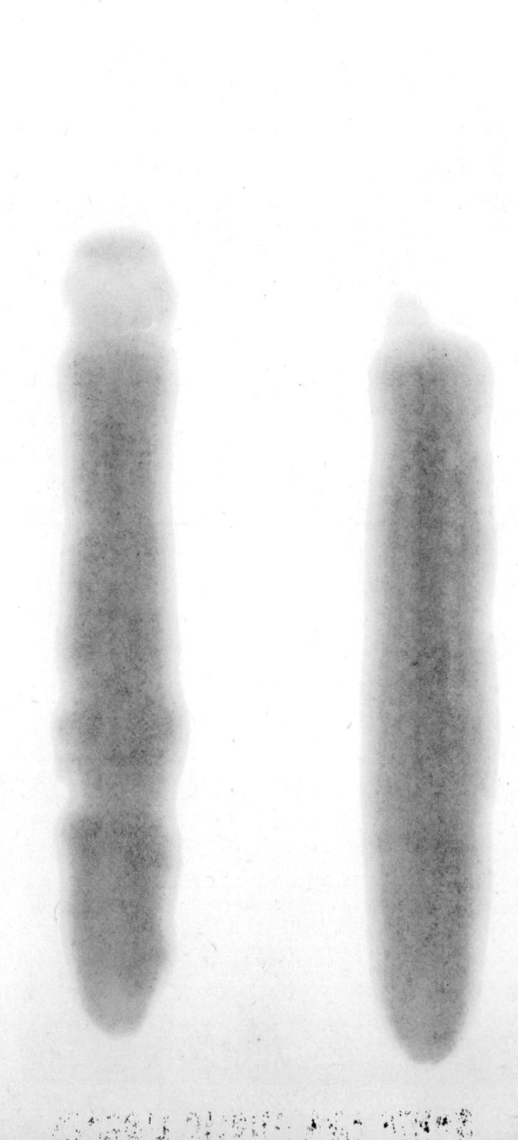

TOULOUSE LAUTREC

By RENATA NEGRI

AVENEL BOOKS
NEW YORK

First U.S. Edition published 1979 by Avenel Books
distributed by Crown Publishers Inc.
Printed in Italy by Fabbri Editori, Milan.
a b c d e f g h i

Traslation by MARY LEE GRISANTI

Library of Congress Cataloging in Publication Data
Negri, Renata.
Toulouse-Lautrec.
1. Toulouse-Lautrec Monfa, Henri Marie Raymond de, 1864-1901.
2. Painters-France-Biography.
ND553.T7N3713 1979 760'.092'4 78-71514
ISBN 0-517-277921

Henri Marie Raymond de Toulouse-Lautrec Monfa was born on November 24, 1864, in Albi in the South of France, the child of first cousins who were descendants of two of the most ancient and noble families in France. His father was the sophisticated Count Alphonse de Toulouse-Lautrec, whose name had been famous since the Crusades, and who divided his time between the delights of the Parisian demi monde and passionate bouts of hunting on the vast family estate. The artist's mother, Adèle Tapié de Céleyran, on the other hand, was a woman of solid principles, deeply religious, austere, yet sweet to those around her. She would always symbolize for Toulouse-Lautrec a safe harbor from life's storms; he would return to her for support in each of his moments of crisis.

Toulouse-Lautrec's serene childhood was marked by happy times, childish amusements, and his first studies, undertaken at one of the family estates, the Château du Bosc, near Albi. In 1873 the family moved to Paris, and he was sent to the Lycée Fontanes, where he exhibited remarkable promise. Two years later, because of delicate health, he was forced to withdraw from the school and pursue his studies with a private tutor.

The boy's interests are revealed in his notebooks, where with increasing frequency diligent translations of Latin and English are interspersed with quick and lively sketches, fragmentary reflections of what he saw around him. The drawings of horses and the caricatures of his teachers and friends testify to his astonishing talent. But for the young heir of the Lautrec family, this artistic calling would not be allowed to progress beyond a pleasurable and elegant dilettantism. Painting had always been among the favorite hobbies of the Lautrec ancestors.

Then two sudden and tragic accidents within a short space of time turned Toulouse-Lautrec's young life upside down and destined him for a course very different from the one that would have been his by birth and temperament.

In May 1878, while he was at home in Albi, Toulouse-Lautrec slipped and broke his left thighbone; a year later, while still recuperating in Barèges, he fell and badly fractured his right thighbone. His fate was irrevocably sealed. The extended suffering, the slow healing, the endless days passed at a variety of hot springs all ended with the certainty that his poor young legs would never grow again. Imprisoned in bed for long intervals, deprived of those things he loved most – games, sports, the wild, happy outdoor world of children – he was tortured by intense physical pain and humiliated by the consciousness of his deformity.

It was a particularly ironic deformity. On the fragile legs of a child there had rapidly developed the robust torso of a man, giving him a peculiar, almost bestial appearance, at the same time pathetic and grotesque. Toulouse-Lautrec reacted with extraordinary strength of character to this special cruelty. In drawing he found a force to conquer his depression and to diminish the boredom of his long hours of immobility. Encouraged by René Princeteau, a deaf-mute painter who was a friend of Count Alphonse, he sought to dedicate himself to painting. At the request of his mother, he first took his degree at the University of Toulouse. But the instant he was free, he set out toward what had been preordained as his direction in life: to become a painter.

After a short apprenticeship with Princeteau, in 1882 he entered the studio of Léon Bonnat. Bonnat was one of those painters favored by the official French art establishment of the time and thus very much in vogue in Paris. Lautrec remained with him for a year, returning to Albi in the summer and painting portraits that demonstrated his fast-growing technical process. When he came back to Paris, he went into the studio of Fernand Cormon, where he studied for another two years and made a number of friends among his fellow art students. In 1886, the year of his meeting with Van Gogh, he outfitted his own studio in Montmartre, where he would stay until 1897. He was on his own for the first time in his life, and though he does not seem to have been affected by any great events or notable changes, his life was rich with small, significant episodes.

Toulouse-Lautrec discovered his own world in the bohemian quarter of Montmartre – in its night spots, in its brothels, in its ballrooms, in its cafés – where a mixture of eccentric people lived tempestuously on the edges of society. Here he was able to live easily; no one cared about or even noticed his deformity. Life was frenetic, carefree, thoughtless, sometimes bitter, but he found it an inexhaustible source for his lively curiosity and his insatiable drawing pencil. In 1893 at the Goupil Gallery he had a show of those of his works that had been inspired by Montmartre, and although it had only a faint success, it won him the approval of the great Degas.

The theatre also began to attract him, and he created many programs and posters for plays and dedicated several paintings to famous actors and actresses. His friend Tristan Bernard introduced him to the realm of sports, where he found additional fascinations and enthusiasms. In 1895 he went to London, where he met Whistler and Oscar Wilde, and in the following year he traveled to Belgium, Spain, and Portugal.

Toulouse-Lautrec began to play an important part in the circles that formed around the Revue Blanche, *which during those years had gathered together the most vital innovators among the Parisian intellectual elite. He made many friends, in particular the Nathanson brothers, who edited the* Revue. *He spent many pleasant weekends at their house in Villeneuve-sur-Yonne, where he was often in the company of artists such as Vallotton, Bonnard, and Vuillard, with whom he shared an intense reciprocal admiration.*

He worked continually at a feverish pace, alternating paintings, posters, cartoons for the newspapers, illustrations for books, and color lithographs. But the abuse of alcohol threatened his life, and in 1899 his mother was forced to commit him to a sanitarium in Neuilly-sur-Seine, where he spent three incredibly sad months. "I am sick", he wrote desperately to his father, "where all who are sick die". To prove to his doctors that he was stable and able to care for himself, he painted from memory a series of scenes inspired by the circus, and largely because of this effort he was granted his freedom. But it was to be short-lived. Notwithstanding the fact that he was accompanied night and day by a sort of bodyguard whose job it was to look after him, he fell prey almost immediately to the turbulence and excess of his old life. The Château de Malromé, in the Gironde, was the refuge where his mother had always soothed him during each of his crises, and it was there that he was struck down by a fatal paralysis in July 1901. On September 9, at the age of thirty-six, his life was brutally cut off, and he died in his mother's arms.

"The difficult, courageous, and sincere act of a man who was fighting for what he loved most-life."

The Drinker or Gueule de Bois - Albi, Musée Toulouse-Lautrec

He passed through our history as the bard of an age: all the frenzy, the ephemeral splendor, the delirious sweetness, the turbulence, and the sadness of that brief and sparkling season we call the *belle époque* can be found in his song. The unique lyric of Henri de Toulouse-Lautrec assures his immortality. Today, when one thinks of the gay and yet squalid Montmartre, of the *fin de siècle* world of the Moulin Rouge and its cancan dancers, the first figure who comes to mind is Toulouse-Lautrec. He has rendered our most faithful and attentive testimony of that world; his art evokes a timeless image of that very special age. More than any other artist of the period, he succeeded in capturing the fleeting impressions of that transitory life, catching the sensation of an everlasting present, the secret life within a human situation that was destined to become eternal.

Free of moral prejudices and rigid cultural precepts of any kind, Toulouse-Lautrec painted because for him it was a vital necessity. Of all the things in his life, it was painting that gave him joy. "I have never put anything before the pleasure of painting," he often told his friends.

During the last fifteen years of the nineteenth century the turbulent, chaotic flux of artistic change raged like a wildfire in Paris. Impressionism, which had begun – all of a sudden, it seemed – with the Exposition of 1874, was already a *fait accompli*, an indispensable premise to creation, but insuffcent in itself to stimulate further new results. The young clamored for new ideas, but they were trapped and frustrated by the stubborn incomprehension of the public and the official critics. They ventured away from the mainstream courageously, with all the ardor of revolutionaries, seeking new poetic visions and experimenting with new techniques and new styles. Cézanne, Gauguin, Van Gogh, and Seurat were the greatest – though as yet unknown. They were the leading figures of the day, coming up beside those great masters of Impressionism who still remained on the scene: Renoir, Monet, Degas, Pissarro. In the studios and cafés frequented by the younger artists, the air was thick with polemicas. They spoke of symbolism. They argued in defense of the *cloisonisme* of Bernard and Gauguin (a technique of compartmentalizing, or cloistering each individual component of the painting as separate from the rest). And they argued in defense of the divisionism of Seurat.

Among so many inflexible schools of thought, so many categorical statements, so much revolutionary fervor, Toulouse-Lautrec did not adhere to any one movement, nor did he ascribe to the philosophy of any particular school. He stood alone, isolated an independent. He never subjugated the greatness of his instinct to theoretical preoccupations. Too modest to separate himself in any obvious way from the master innovators of his time, he treated them with sincere and enthusiastic admiration. He was, in fact, especially dedicated to the quiet and subtle genius of Degas. It is to him that Toulouse-Lautrec's art owes perhaps its greatest debt, particularly if one looks at certain intellectual stimuli that many of their themes and even their stylistic language have in common.

Toulouse-Lautrec had attempted to pay his tribute to the Impressionists in his youthful portraits by painting outdoors. Yet without his ever actually insisting that the course of the Impressionists was not compatible with his own, it seems relatively clear that he was affected for the most part not by them but by Degas, by the Japanese prints that were so popular at that time, and indirectly by the artistic ambience of Paris. He had an emotional capacity that enabled him to translate through stylistic suggestion a mode that was destined to become profound and meditative. Degas had been fascinated by the world of the theater, and explored that world in his paintings, being especially attentive to the humblest considerations of its daily life. He was able to capture exactly the effort in the contorted gestures of his figures and create a series of intense, unconventional snapshots, each one reflecting a real moment. The legacy of Hiroshige and Uttamaro and the other Japanese masters was the perfectly controlled capriciousness of line, an elegance in drawing that is able to recreate a personality and an ambience against an essence of contour. They brought to the West a novelty of compositional cut and perspective, obtained by juxtaposing planes, which accent the figure in the foreground.

Toulouse-Lautrec was affected by all these elements to varying degrees as he struggled to formulate his own mature style. He reworked them into a personal vision that appears from a distance to owe its stylistic perfection and decorative elegance to Degas's abstracting of Japanese compositions, but which is ultimately unique.

Toulouse-Lautrec's vocation was derived from inward sorrow, from the impossibility of his leading a normal life, from his painful physical imprisonment. His sources of inspiration were to be found in the world outside himself – in exuberance, in opulence, in the constant variety of life that he saw moving rapidly around him. His painting owes everything to that vital pulse, made of gesture and feeling, of the moment, of the immediate, and of the changing. His gift is both humorous and pathetic, concise and quintessential, and, above all, passionate. His sensitivity to line is sharp, fluid, agile, and extraordinarily expressive. His economy is also remarkable; he achieves effects of surprising novelty through the use of only a few pure colors, especially in the posters and color lithographs. The success of his posters was rapid and widespread. His first public posters, plastered all over the streets of Paris, were shocking in their obvious and liberal realism and in the originality of their design (for instance, showing only half a figure). The open challenge in the posters did more than any movement or polemic to work against the conventions of taste, the prejudices, and the shabby prudery of bourgeois society. All Paris was either enthusiastic about or scandalized by his posters as they went up, one after the other.

In this genre, as in his paintings of horse races, Toulouse-Lautrec was no one's disciple – or not, at any rate, a proper pupil in the sense of having had a master – though perhaps he was marginally influenced by Rouault. He invented a new way of dealing with graphics, which he has bequeathed to contemporary art, giving us both a testimony and an inheritance.

His was a bizarre and, no doubt, cruel fate. He had been given genius and an insatiable thirst for life and for knowledge. He had also been given his deformity; that grotesque and sorrowful form which only the splendor of his great and melancholy eyes saved from appearing ridiculous. To escape depression and the pity that

The Laundress - Cleveland, Museum of Art, donation of Hanua Fund

the well-meaning, well-born world around him could not help but inflict upon him, he took refuge in Montmartre. This was a carefree bohemian neighborhood, not yet overrun by tourists, which thrived on the fringes of the law. It was equally hospitable to vice and to art, to an hour's pleasure or the long, slow demise of an entire life. It was the world of Montmartre, emerging each evening from the squalid poverty of day to be draped in gaudy lights and transformed with joyful and seductive spectacles in a hundred little dance halls, that Toulouse-Lautrec set out to explore. He found in Montmartre an inexhaustible wealth of personalities and types, capable of reawakening all his curiosity and interests. Here were characters to study patiently, to analyze endlessly in order to extract some essence of expression that would ever after be recognized as their most human, most *real* truth. To them Toulouse-Lautrec dedicated his artistic tribute: an acute impartial portrait, as free from criticism as it is free from complacency, sometimes veiled by a shadow of tenderness or faintly stained with polite irony, but in every case completely human. The life that had consigned him to the role of spectator could not harden his heart, nor could it dry up his spirit.

At the age of five Toulose-Lautrec's favorite game was making little portraits, from life, with his colored pencils. He drew the various people and animals that populated his serene childhood world. After his second accident, when it became clear that he would never again be a boy like other boys, drawing became a pleasurable escape from the intolerable demands of his daily routine. He loved the life of free movement – the races, hunting, games. During the endless days of recuperation, when time passed so slowly that it seemed almost to stand still in the four corners of his room, when his only escape was the view from his window, his artistic bent deepened. Instead of an escape, art became a courageous as well as pathetic attempt to revive on paper what life would no longer allow him.

His album from Nizza, in 1880, contains numerous sketches of sailors, ships, carriages, and horses. The technique is biting, if the knowledge of perspective and anatomy is still uncertain. These sketches astonish us with their extraordinary synthesis, mixing a nervous agility, temper, and an overbearing force, with a concentrated and vital fullness of gesture. To Toulouse-Lautrec gesture meant that small, fleeting movement that defines a character and a moment. And therein lay his power, from his adolescent drawings to his mature paintings. It is a dynamic synthesis that transforms his subject into a rapid signature, throwing out everything that is superfluous, and keeping only what is quintessential. Thus he powerfully reduces his subject to maximum expressive potential.

René Princeteau, who often visited the Lautrec family, was entirely won by the boy's talents and did much to help him acquire technical refinements, bringing him to Paris and taking him into his own studio for the spring of 1882. But Lautrec's curiosity was already reaching beyond the world of Princeteau. During that summer he traveled back and forth between the Château du Bosc (the Lautrec estate) and the home of the Céleyrans, his mother's family. And all that time his interest was absorbed by the people – acquaintances, peasant farmers, field hands – whom he was able to observe at their daily tasks. He did many fine and intense portraits out in the fields, using a technique of little crisscrossing touches of color. Already he was handling color capably, researching the effects of changing light and revealing, perhaps unwittingly his interest in and link to the Impressionists.

His next apprenticeship was in the studio of that academic painter of the old school, Léon Bonnat. There he was obliged to study the inflexible rules of the Academy, and this seemed to induce him to negate those qualities in his own style that were the most authentic and most alive. However, the portrait of his mother, done in the summer of 1883, shows subtle variations of white and gives preeminence to the foreground, accenting the blue cup and the great hands of the countess. This attempt to interpret a subject in a totally real way testifies to the progressive maturity of his vision.

The effort to animate his drawing in a way that would follow all the rules and make it utterly, technically correct – an effort that Toulouse-Lautrec submitted to patiently in the studio of Fernand Cormon – could not suffocate his vision. It was the forging of a strong stylistic tool that he would use freely for his own deeply personal ends.

An instinctive distaste for the style of official painting, together with a proclivity for the comic and for caricature, characterizes the work of Toulouse-Lautrec even in the years he spent in Cormon's studio. He expresses himself quite clearly in his parody of Puvis de Chavannes's "The Sacred Woods," shown at the Salon in 1884. Cormon, and academic painting in general, had little to teach Toulouse-Lautrec. The artist kept on searching, as he always would, for his own direction.

Finally, enthusiastically championing Degas and yet bent on finding his own dream, Toulouse-Lautrec went to live in the midst of the most cataclysmic artistic ferment of the day – among the young artists of Montmartre. Between 1885 and 1888 he did a series of drawings and paintings (among which the portraits are most noteworthy) in which he seemed to be slowly piecing together the language that would become uniquely his. Little by little he gathered the suggestions and influences of others and made of them a personal, interpretative method that he could apply as spontaneously as his own sight. In 1886 Toulouse-Lautrec met Van Gogh, toward whom he had developed an instinctive sympathy, and the portrait he dedicated to him a year later reveals in its rapid, almost violent lines that Toulouse-Lautrec shared a deep, perhaps subconscious understanding with Van Gogh. But he treated the meeting as an episode, an isolated fact that led to nothing beyond itself.

In fact, even the Impressionists did not have a much more substantial or long-lived effect upon him. It appears with increasing clarity that the actual difference between Toulouse-Lautrec and the Impressionists is this: although they both observed their subjects in the natural environment, as part of a daily ambience, Lautrec made little or nothing at all of the changes in the atmosphere. Among all his concerns, he concentrated most on the human presence. This dominates all his paintings, bringing an expression to life in a single gesture. Of the portraits he painted between 1888 and 1891, many are situated in public gardens. There is a breakthrough in their brief abstracting and comprehensive style. He reduced everything to a speckled thicket of color against which the figure in the foreground is

At La Mie - Boston, Museum of Fine Arts

accented in a clear, still light that brings every detail into sharp focus.

In 1888 there appeared another painting of historical importance: "The Fernando Circus". "The Bareback Rider", which, in fact, introduced a new genre and a new technique – a vision of life as scenes from a circus – Toulouse-Lautrec presented for the first time the elements that are most original and most animated in his artistic vocabulary. The point of view moves across different planes of action. Figures are held in their own dynamic and transient reality, somewhat like silhouettes in their simplification of an already reductive design, brought down to a single fluid, rhythmic line. And his color has been boiled down to an equally basic and elementary palette. These qualities are the hallmarks of his mature style. Toulouse-Lautrec had only to look around and choose his subjects from the never-ending real-life circus of Montmartre, which seemed to mirror the life throbbing inside him. These people were not strangers whose bizarre appearance caught the eye of the artist. They were, quite simply, his friends.

From 1886 on he favored the celebrated singer and composer Aristide Bruant above all others, spending many of his evenings in Bruant's cabaret Le Mirliton and illustrating several sheet music covers for him. But there were other famous night spots where one could find the small gentleman, always impeccably dressed, whose drawings amused the local clientele: Le Moulin de la Galette, Le Bal Elysée Montmartre, and – in 1889, the year that it opened – Le Moulin Rouge. Here the young laundresses and dressmakers' assistants dazzled the night with the exuberance of their youth, dancing a frenetic, almost violent new dance that was to become famous throughout the world – the cancan. Here life was irrepressible, exploding in a thousand sparkling and unexpected ways. And it was here that Toulouse-Lautrec found his most important clues to life's seductive and elusive mysteries. Sitting for hours at a little table, pad and pencil in front of him, he sketched quickly and surely, capturing the multiplicity of images in the human comedy around him, a drama acted by real people and set in the thick of a warm steam of alcohol. These were fleeting moments, and he captured their essence on canvas and in lithographs.

His first poster, in 1889, was for Le Moulin Rouge. It pictured La Goulue, the coarse provincial girl who had become their prima ballerina and whose form seemed magically transformed at the first note she sang, changing until she was one with her dance, indistinguishable from the music. In her Toulouse-Lautrec saw not only a symbol but the concrete incarnation of a vital, collective desire. La Goulue, with her leg proudly raised, her young body taut and vibrant as a bow, provoking and challenging, was for Toulouse-Lautrec a triumphant affirmation of life.

Many other figures moved across Toulouse-Lautrec's horizon, and he succeeded in highlighting in each the most personal and most significant characteristics. He restored their integrity with the touch of his pen and with the restrained yet friendly and pervasive mark of his colors. Spectacles of any kind exerted an irresistible fascination for him – from the late-night cafés of Montmartre to the great playhouses of the Champs Elysées, from the race-tracks to the sports arenas, with their rivalry and fierce competition – and he captured this excitement in his drawings. He seemed consumed by a kind of fever as he sat night after night in the public Jardin de Paris, reinterpreting the image of Jane Avril again and again in the same compositions. He also returned to the

Divan Japonais to record the fantastic mobility of expression of the disquieting and enigmatic young actress Yvette Guilbert. Of Guilbert he has left images that are a testament to dramatic intelligence.

He saw in the female clown Cha-U-Kao the consciousness of human pain. In the shameless yellow of her ballooning Pierrot costume and in the shadow of her eyes, which brimmed with tenderness, he found a resigned and pathetic melancholy. In the face of Marcelle Lender, pictured during a bolero dance of Chilpéric's, he transformed each sensation into luminous fireworks of color. The splendor of her thick hair, the pink dots and green stripes of her blouse, contrast with the blue suits of the pageboys to animate the composition with the unique impulse of her dance.

And it is with equal incisiveness, almost forcing reality to cut itself open and expose its own entrails, that Toulouse-Lautrec drew the figures of some of the popular personalities of the circus (especially the clowns Footit and Chocolat), the habitués of various Montmartre haunts, his own friends (such as his distant cousin Gabriel Tapié de Céleyran), and nameless people he spotted in the crowd whose profiles or expressions or particular gestures happened to attract the eye of the artist.

He also had a sincere and intense curiosity about the world of prostitutes, and he drew them without prejudice and without sentimentality, taking interest in the candor of their very human situation. Toulouse-Lautrec, who had always despised paintings composed in the studio because of the falseness inherent in posing, created inside the brothels his most beautiful studies of nudes and many of his most truthful portraits. These were the fruit of an intimacy that was part of their daily life and that completely ignored complacency as it ignored distaste. Toulouse-Lautrec's pen purified whatever subject it touched, even the most scabrous. He never judged or condemned, but was able to rescue in every human gesture, including those of vice and abnormality, that particle of truth that renders the *real*.

Between 1889 and 1899 Lautrec's art, characterized by this multiplicity of themes, enjoyed its happiest season, maintaining almost the same stylistic vocabulary and conserving a constant level of prodigious and expressive intensity. His compositions were articulated through unusual perspectives. The contours were clean and aggressive. The colors – always few and pure – were becoming milder and clearer, creating a more subtle and suggestive mood. The pink bodice of May Belfort contrasting with the piercing blue she wears underneath, and the red-brown hair of "Madame Poulpoule à la Toilette" against the iridescent green of her bathrobe with its crystal buttons are notable examples of this.

By 1899 the instability of Toulouse-Lautrec's life style and his abuse of alcohol were threatening his life. After a particularly violent crisis he was sent by his family to a sanitarium, where he tried to revive his joie de vivre and regain his sense of security by executing a series of drawings on the circus. But something was exhausted in him, perhaps his most passionate curiosity about life, which had imposed its extraordinary character on the works he had done up until this time.

When he left the clinic, weak and ill, he had all but given up the use of pencil and of pen and ink, though there is no lack of authentic masterpieces from even this most extreme period in his life; witness the portrait of a young English girl he had met in a bar in Le Havre. It is possible to find in these works a residue of his best qualities, and also an expressive insecurity that led him to experiment with yet more new techniques and to widen his stylistic vocabulary. "An Exam at the Medical School," executed in 1901, substitutes heavy masses of color for the graphic value of the images; perhaps it is indicative of the beginning of a new phase in Toulouse-Lautrec's painting. But there was no further development; death overtook him only a few months later.

It is the Lautrec of "At the Moulin Rouge," and of "Au Salon de la Rue des Moulins" (the most impressive of the paintings inspired by the brothels) and the Toulouse-Lautrec of the thousand ironic and pathetic portraits to whom we must turn again before passing judgment. For us, his unprejudiced and non conformist paintings have come to symbolize the realization of the poet's calling. They must, in the last analysis, represent the difficult, courageous, and sincere act of a man who was fighting for what he loved most – life.

Index of the illustrations

I - Self-portrait - Oil on board, 1880 - Albi, France, Musée Henri de Toulouse-Lautrec - *Done at the age of seventeen, this portrait is testimony to the artist's precocity. His sense of his calling, present from childhood, was affirmed with energy and originality until the end of life.*

II - Alphonse de Toulouse-Lautrec-Monfa - 1881 - Paris, Musée de Petit Palais - *In this early portrait of his father, Toulouse-Lautrec's characteristic style, in which details are impossible to define precisely, is already evident.*

III - The Countess of Toulouse-Lautrec at Lunch - 1883 - Albi, France, Musée Henri de Toulouse-Lautrec - *This portrait of the artist's mother was painted at Malromé one summer when he was studying with Bonnat. The large, simplified visual planes of her form accentuate her severe, pensive expression.*

IV-V - Rachous, the Painter - 1882 - Dallas, Collection of Algur H. Meadows - *Although still following the methods of his teacher, Cormon, Toulouse-Lautrec was now coming into contact with other students. This painting shows the influence of his increasingly important association with that enclave of young artists who were to emerge as the major forces of modern French art.*

VI - The Slow Horse - 1881 - Paris, Private collection - *Toulouse-Lautrec's first mentor was René Princeteau, a family friend and one of the greatest painters of horses. While studying with Pinceteau, he did many equine studies as well as studies of jockeys, races, and numerous animals.*

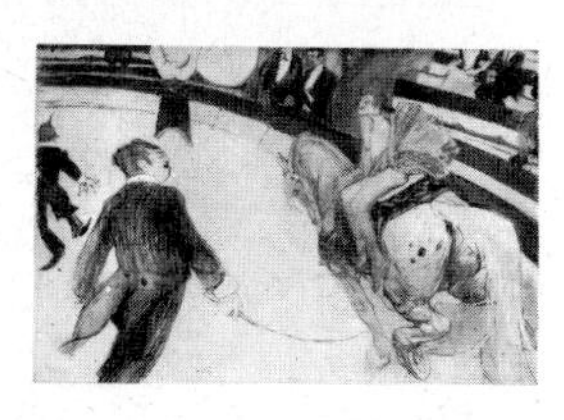

VII - The Fernand Circus: The Bareback Rider - 1880 - The Art Institute of Chicago - *This is one of the earliest paintings in which the artist's expressive force and innovative intelligence (in terms of composition) are evident.*

VIII - Portrait of Vincent Van Gogh - 1887 - Amsterdam, Collection of the Vincent Van Gogh Foundation - *While studying with Cormon, Toulouse-Lautrec frequently encountered Van Gogh, and a deep friendship grew between the two artists. This portrait is unusual in its emotional intensity.*

IX - The Last Drop - Pencil and watercolor, 1886 - Private collection - *Toulouse-Lautrec was fascinated with personalities in which vice or weakness played a major role, and he immortalized them in his art. This portrayal of a bizarre segment of society is a vivid example of his unceasing interest in everything human.*

X - The Laundress - 1889 - Paris, Private collection - *Desiring to capture ordinary life, Toulouse-Lautrec scorned professional models. This girl is simply a worker who caught the artist's eye as he passed her on the street.*

XI - Girl with Red Hair - 1889 - Zurich, Switzerland, Private collection - *This is one of many portraits of women that the artist painted in the public garden in Montmartre. The natural background is of decorative value only, but the girl's expression is a study in subtle sensitivity.*

XII - Portrait of Helene Vary - 1888 - Bremen, Germany, Kunsthalle - *The portraits reveal more clearly than any other aspect of his painting the fundamental difference between Toulouse-Lautrec and the other Impressionists. He was not interested in the changing effects of light in nature, but rather devoted himself to man and the environment that man had created for himself.*

XIII - The Countess Adèle Tapié de Céleyran de Toulouse-Lautrec in the Salon of the Château de Malromé - Albi, France, Musée Henri de Toulouse-Lautrec - *This portrait of the artist's mother shows a moment of simple domestic intimacy. The environmental details are used to heighten the effect of the psychological content of the portrait.*

XIV - Aristide Bruant in His Cabaret - 1893 - Albi, France, Musée Henri de Toulouse-Lautrec - *Toulouse-Lautrec, famed for his posters, revolutionized the use of the foreground. In this example the poet Bruant is in his cabaret, where the most vital artistic personalities of the day often gathered.*

XV - Aristide Bruant at Les Ambassadeurs - 1892 - Albi, France, Musée Henri de Toulouse-Lautrec - *Emphasis on the human form is characteristic of Toulouse-Lautrec's work, and it is the human presence that gives this poster its power.*

XVI - Jane Avril at the Jardin de Paris - Albi, France, Musée Henri de Toulouse-Lautrec - *The artist's interest in Japanese prints, which were extremely popular in Paris at the time, is shown in the elegance of this illustration. His originality and inventiveness—especially the manipulation of the foreground—force the viewer to "frame" the image of the dancers.*

XVII - Divan Japonais - 1892 - Paris, Bibliothèque Nationale - *Artistic vigor and quick insight are evidenced in this poster in which the central figure seems to be caught in the middle of an action, almost as in a photograph. The simplicity of the color scheme accents the vitality of the scene.*

XVIII - Candy - Albi, France, Musée Henri de Toulouse-Lautrec - *Because the poster form demands an immediate and striking image, Toulouse-Lautrec's experience in designing posters gave him the opportunity to develop fully his agile and expressive line.*

XIX - Miss May Belfort - 1891 - Paris, Bibliothèque Nationale - *This poster shows how the artist was able to transmit a potent image by using only a few lines and strong primary colors.*

XX - The Troupe of Mlle Eglantine - Turin, Italy, Private collection - *In this simple drawing in neutral tones Toulouse-Lautrec uses only a few rapid pencil strokes and a touch of gesso to convey economically the frenzied movement of the cancan dancers.*

XXI - Jane Avril Dancing at the Moulin Rouge - Paris, Jeu de Paume - *Jane Avril, one of the few friends among the many showgirls and actresses Toulouse-Lautrec painted, was a favorite subject. He found her subtle melancholy expression appealing and responded to her sensitivity and air of refinement which contrasted sharply with the other popular stars of the day, notably La Goulue.*

XXII - Woman Drinking - Pen and ink, 1889 - Albi, France, Musée Henri de Toulouse-Lautrec - *This drawing, a portrait of Suzanne Valadon, a popular artists' model, demonstrates Toulouse-Lautrec's ability to convey the complex personality of a subject by emphasizing only a few carefully chosen characteristics.*

XXIII - Woman Dancing - 1890 - Paris, Private collection - *This sketch, typical of the artist's spare use of color at the time, achieves a sense of space with only a few basic tones. Gradually he opened up his canvases and used brighter and brighter colors.*

XXIV-XXV - The Moulin Rouge - 1892 - The Art Institute of Chicago - *Inside the famous club Moulin Rouge each individual has a story: the nightclub habitués at the left, La Goulue, the local dancers with their backs to the mirror, the girl on the right, covered with sparkling blue light.*

XXVI - The Moulin Rouge - The Art Institute of Chicago - *Montmartre at night was one of Toulouse-Lautrec's favorite subjects, and he always treated the joyous and exuberant world there in surprising ways. Here, for example, the features of the clientele are distorted by the myriad reflections of the stage lights.*

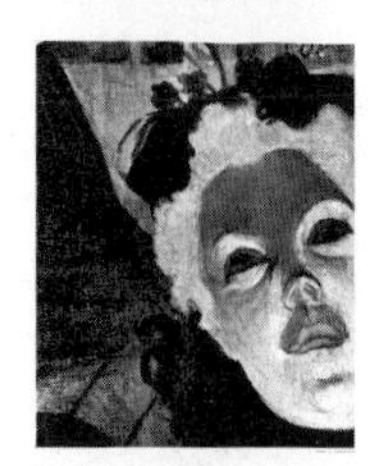

XXVII - The Moulin Rouge - The Art Institute of Chicago - *Here foreshortening brings the viewer forcibly into that seductive spectacle that held such a keen attraction for Toulouse-Lautrec.*

XXVIII - Bal au Moulin de la Gallette - 1889 - The Art Institute of Chicago, Collection of Mr. and Mrs. Lewis L. Coburn - *In this work the viewer has the sensation of entering the dance. Toulouse-Lautrec achieved this effect by placing a spectator in the foreground of the painting, thus bridging the gap between the viewer and the action.*

XXIX - Portrait of Samary of the Comédie-Française - 1889 - Paris, Collection of J. Laroche - *In this fantastic work the artist has a very personal means of capturing just those attributes of his subject's personality that are most revealing—analyzing his movement and portraying an aura.*

XXX - Mr. Warner at the Moulin Rouge - 1892 - New York, Metropolitan Museum of Art, bequest of Miss Adelaide Milton de Groot, New York - *Toulouse-Lautrec left an impressive gallery of psychological studies, of which this drawing is a fine example. Each of them captures a different fact of human character.*

XXXI - La Goulue at the Moulin Rouge - 1892 - New York, Museum of Modern Art, Gift of Mrs. David M. Levy - *Toulouse-Lautrec's genius for poster design helped to create the immense success and popularity of La Goulue, bringing her exuberant image to every street corner in Paris.*

XXXII - Yvette Guilbert - Paris, Bibliothèque Nationale - *An actress, singer and dancer, Guilbert was a close friend of the artist. In the 1890's he dedicated his most successful albums of drawings to her.*

XXXIII - Profile of a Woman - Paris, Private collection - *Part of a series done in the 1890's, this drawing is an excellent example of Toulouse-Lautrec's exceptional ability to capture a personality with a few quick lines.*

XXXIV - Jane Avril Leaves the Moulin Rouge - 1892 - Hartford, Connecticut, Wadsworth Atheneum - *When her popularity, which had been bolstered by the artist's many posters, drawings, and lithographs of her, finally waned, Jane Avril was practically thrown out of the Moulin Rouge onto the streets. In this drawing the quality of pathos is heightened by the halo of light around her.*

XXXV - The Dance of La Goulue - 1895 - Paris, Musée National du Louvre - *The second of the two panels, done for what La Goulue called her "Barracks"; the dancer is here positioned in the foreground among her friends. The effect is to pull the viewer into the painting.*

XXXVI - Woman of the House - 1894 - Private collection - *During Toulouse-Lautrec's time Montmartre was one of the poorest quarters in Paris. He did many portraits revealing the degradation of the people living there.*

XXXVII - Miss May Belfort - 1895 - Paris, Private collection - *May Belfort, a singer of Irish background, caught the eye of the artist from the audience at the Moulin Rouge. He painted her as she sang, in an act in which she held a black cat.*

XXXVIII - Caudieux - Albi, France, Musée Henri de Toulouse-Lautrec - *Here the artist uses an opaque background and quickly renders, in chiaroscuro, a person in mid-action.*

XXXIX - Redoute au Moulin Rouge - Albi, France, Musée Henri de Toulouse-Lautrec - *The famous nightclub, which opened in 1889 and became an overnight success, provided Toulouse-Lautrec with an almost inexhaustible source of inspiration. He was intrigued both by the performers and the audience, a mix of many types—from dancers, actors and acrobats, to voyeurs—and their follies.*

XL - La Goulue Valse - 1894 - Albi, France, Musée Henri de Toulouse-Lautrec - *At the age of twenty-seven, Toulouse-Lautrec began to design posters, soon distinguishing himself with his revolutionary style. All his life he ignored the "beautiful picture" style of advertising and concentrated on projecting a true image of the subject, as is apparent here.*

XLI - Moulin Rouge: La Goulue - 1891 - Albi, France, Musée Henri de Toulouse-Lautrec - *As with so many of his posters, here the artist involves the viewer in the scene he is observing. This is achieved by the profile of the dancer in the foreground, which draws the onlooker into the world of the painting.*

XLII - Dance at the Moulin Rouge - 1890 - Philadelphia, Henry P. McIlhuny Collection - *Here Toulouse-Lautrec vividly conveys the atmosphere of the Moulin Rouge and convinces us of its attractions for the dancers, the artists, and the local habitués who congregated there.*

XLIII - The Clowness Cha-U-Kao - Winterthur, Switzerland, Reinhart Collection - *In this perfectly balanced composition the appealingly gaudy figure of Cha-U-Kao dominates the scene. Extraordinary in its chromatic balance, the yellows and browns are in counterpoint in the foreground, and the pink bouquet of the dress at the left contrasts with the sharp green of the background.*

XLIV - Yvette Guilbert Greets Her Public - Albi, France, Musée Henri de Toulouse-Lautrec - *Having met the actress in 1894, Toulouse-Lautrec never ceased to admire her prodigious talent as an actress, her gift for irony, and her capacity for friendship with all types of people. He studied her for a long time and made numerous portraits of her in an attempt to convey the disquieting enigma of her personality.*

XLV - Yvette Guilbert - Albi, France, Musée Henri de Toulouse-Lautrec - *Although she did not at first approve of his interest in her, the artist dedicated an entire series of posters to Guilbert, and as his work helped to create her extraordinary success, she began to appreciate his friendship and the fact that his brilliant rendering of her was the most subtle interpretation of her personality.*

XLVI-XLVII - Au Salon à la Rue des Moulins - 1894 - Albi, France, Musée Henri de Toulouse-Lautrec - *Among the artist's many works inspired by the life of the prostitutes, this example is the most impressive. In the vast salon, painted in violent colors, a dense, almost suffocating atmosphere prevails. Among the girls lying on the divans is the rigid figure of the madam, her face acutely characterized.*

XLVIII - The Bed - 1894 - Paris, Musée National du Louvre - *This strikingly simple painting is an example of Toulouse-Lautrec's concern for the intimate human environment, as apposed to the passion for the natural environment of most Impressionists.*

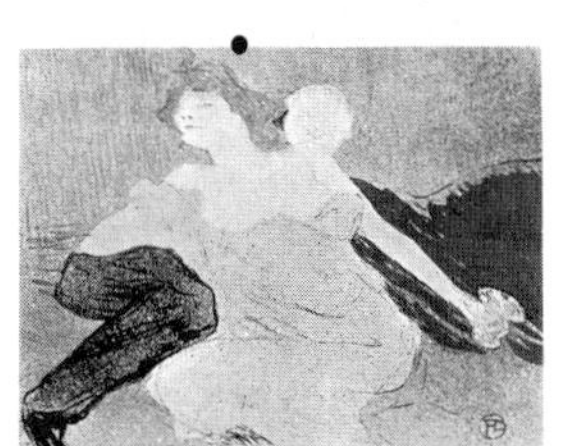

XLIX - Debauche - Lithograph - *Without giving way to vulgarity or licentiousness, the artist concentrates on the personalities and events of the "Salon", the famous Montmartre brothel. He distills in the expressions the essence of each individual and presents these people and their situation without prejudice.*

L - Loie Fuller - Paris, Private collection - *For Loie Fuller, who was the most original of the dancers painted by Toulouse-Lautrec, the artist devised a new method of lithography: color was applied directly to the paper and the image was later dusted with gold powder. The effect was of lines and colors fusing as if melted together.*

LI - Dr. Gabriel Tapié de Céléyran - 1894 - Albi, France, Musée Henri de Toulouse-Lautrec - *In this portrait of his cousin the artist complements his characteristic economy of line with an unprecedented use of color.*

LII - Suffit (The Good Jockey) - Illustration, 1895 - Le Figaro Illustré, July - *During a period of heightened productivity from 1890to 1900, Toulouse-Lautrec did many illustrations for newspapers and books, of which this is an example.*

LIII - Chocolat Dances in the Bar d'Achille - 1896 - Albi, France, Musée Henri de Toulouse-Lautrec - *Exhibited with a group of works depicting the simultaneously gay and lurid world of Montmartre, this drawing captures both the vitality and the anxiety of the scene. The viewer participates in the intense emotion of the work.*

LIV - A la Toilette - Paris, Musée National du Louvre - *The artist named this woman "Solitude" and, with characteristic feeling and perception, grasped her profound desolation.*

LV - Marcelle Lender Dances Chilperic's Bolero Dance - New York, Collection of J. H. Whitney - *Toulouse-Lautrec was so mesmerized by Marcelle Lender's interpretation of Chilperic's operetta that he returned to the theater night after night to sketch her during the show. He made hundreds of studies and sketches which retain the explosive rhythm and color of her dancing.*

LVI - Mme Poupoule à la Toilette - 1898 - Albi, France, Musée Henri de Toulouse-Lautrec - *This exquisite painting reveals the artist's full maturity, in both his imaginative use of color and his exceptional sensitivity toward the subject and her ambience.*

LVII - L'Assommoir - 1900 - Collection of Mrs. Florence Gould - *Done in the year before the artist's final collapse, this mural was made for the theatrical production of Emile Zola's L'*Assommoir.

LVIII - The Dance of La Goulue and Valentin le Desossé - Paris, Musée National du Louvre - *Typical of Toulouse-Lautrec's ability to portray pathos in a nonetheless joyous and exciting style, this painting is populated by all the characters he loved—singers, dancers, actors. This duality of effect in his posters and theater illustrations made him very popular.*

LIX - The Dance of La Goulue - Paris, Musée National du Louvre - *This poster of La Goulue, dancing under the flashing spotlights of the Moulin Rouge, was one of the artist's most popular renderings. Rival artists and establishments claimed that his success and the success of the café were a result of the notoriety of the subjects.*

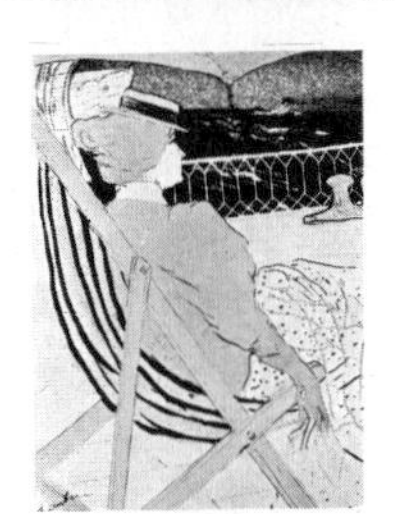

LX - The Unknown Passenger in Cabin 54 - Lithograph, 1896 - *The influence of the innovations of Toulouse-Lautrec on modern advertising graphics is still felt today. His unusual directness of approach to the subject and his concept of minimal line and color are part of today's viewpoint.*

LXI - At the Bar: The Cashier - Zurich, Switzerland, Kunsthaus - *Two anonymous figures in a café are here given immortality by the artist's incredible facility for the quick sketch. Using pen and ink, he seems to paint and sketch simultaneously. There are few characterizations which are as pungent as this heavy face and the woman's sharp profile which emerges from her pale jabot.*

LXII - The English Girl at The Star in Le Havre - Albi, France, Musée Henri de Toulouse-Lautrec - *The Star was a cafè in Le Havre, where the artist met the English girl who inspired this portrait, one of the masterpieces of his last period. He has returned to rapid and incisive lines and aggressive color, quickly filling in a background composed of minimal geometric forms.*

LXIII - An Exam at the Medical School - Albi, France, Musée Henri de Toulouse-Lautrec - *Begun only a few months before he died, this is the last major painting. In it the artist seems to be creating a new technique, comprised of somber visual masses and dense colors. His untimely death has left us with the question of how his style might have developed had he lived on.*

II

VI

IX

X

XII

Nº 52
Aristide Bruant

AMBASSADEURS
aristide
BRUANT
dans
son cabaret
HLautrec

Jane Avril

Divan Japonais
75 rue des Martyrs
Ed Fournier
directeur

Confetti
Manufactured
by
J & E Bella,
113 Charing Cross Rd.
London.
W.C.
imp. Bella & de Malherbe London & Paris

XVIII

May Belfort
Edw. Ancourt. Paris

XX

XXII

XXIII

XXIV

XXVI

XXXI

XXXII

XXXIV

XXXV

XXXVI

XXXVII

XXXVIII

A Monsieur Victor VIGOUREUX
la Goulue
valse pour piano
par
A. BOSC
Tout exemplaire de ce dessin imprimé sans
la musique est la propriété de l'Auteur.
Paris, A. BOSC, Editeur, 8, Rue Rochechouart

LES SOIRS

XLII

XLIV

XLV

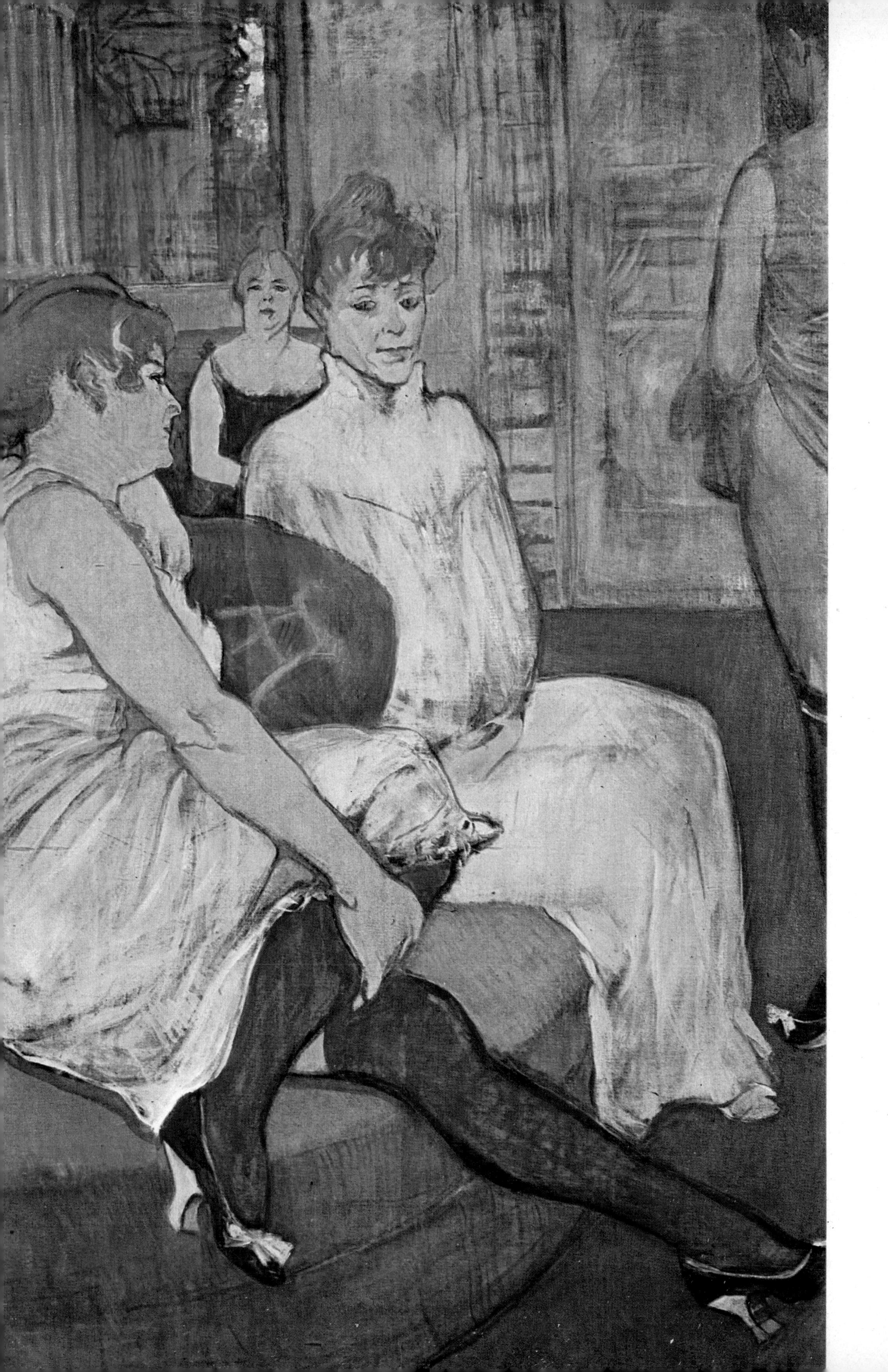

XLVII

XLVIII

XLIX

LI

LIII

LVI

LVIII

HLautrec
1895